Introduction

About your tests

At the end of Year 6, you will take tests to find out about your maths skills. This book will help you revise your **geometry, measures and statistics** skills.

- There will be one **arithmetic** test. This test will ask you to carry out calculations. You will have 30 minutes to do this test.
- There will be two **reasoning** tests. These tests will ask you to solve problems. You will have 40 minutes to do each test.

Using this book

Each page of this book is about a different maths skill. Use the checkboxes at the top of the page to track your progress:

Had a go ☐ Tick this box when you've read the page.

Nearly there ☐ Tick this box when you understand the page quite well.

Nailed it! ☐ Tick this box when you understand the page really well.

Measures   Had a go ☐   Nearly there ☐   Nailed it! ☐

Length

1. Amber and David are siblings.

   David is 1.05 m tall. Amber is 75 cm tall.

   cm to mm × 10
   m to cm × 100
   km to m × 1,000

   a) How tall is David in centimetres?

   1.05 × 100 = 105 cm

   ....105 cm..........   1 mark

   b) Who is the tallest and by how much?

   ....

   ....   1 mark

2. A museum has models of different composers.
   A model of Brahms is 14.5 cm.
   A model of Mozart is 96 mm.
   A model of Beethoven is 0.55 m.
   Write these models in order of size, starting with the smallest.

   ....

   ....   2 marks

3. Joe finds the distance from his home to three places. The nearest post box is 110 m away. The nearest newsagent is 1.1 km away. The nearest dentist is 1,100,000 cm away.

   a) Which of them is closest to Joe's home?

   ....   1 mark

   b) Which of them is furthest from Joe's home?

   ....   1 mark

   c) Which of them is just over one million millimetres away from Joe's home?

   ....   1 mark

Had a go ☐   Nearly there ☐   Nailed it! ☐   **Measures**

Weight

1. A shop sells two types of potatoes.

   | King Edwards 4 kg bag for £5 | Pembrokeshires 2,500 g bag for £5 |

   a) How much are King Edwards per kilogram?

   5 ÷ 4 = 1.25

   (kg to g × 1,000 / t to kg × 1,000)

   ......£1.25...... 1 mark

   b) Convert 2,500 g to kilograms.

   .... 1 mark

   c) How much are Pembrokeshires per kilogram?

   .... 1 mark

2. A shop sells four different types of rice. The bags are different sizes.

   brown rice   650 g   jasmine rice   1.5 kg
   long grain rice   2 kg   basmati rice   1,750 g

   Put the bags in order of their weight, starting with the heaviest.

   ....

   .... 2 marks

3. A garage has two vans for hire. They can hold these weights.

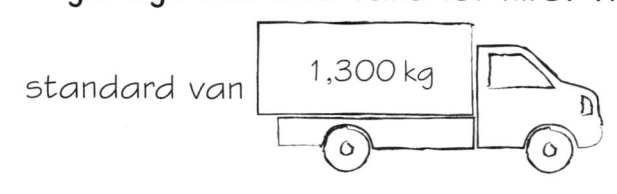

   standard van — 1,300 kg   four-wheel drive van — 1.2 tonnes

   a) Which van can hold the heavier weight, and by how much?

   ....

   .... 2 marks

   b) Another garage has a van that can hold one million grams. Is this more or less than each of the first two vans? By how much?

   ....

   .... 2 marks

Measures — Had a go ☐   Nearly there ☐   Nailed it! ☐

Volume and capacity

1. Xanthe arrives at a petrol station with 17.5 litres of petrol in her car. She buys 20 litres of petrol.

   a) How many litres of petrol are now in her car?

   20 + 17.5 = 37.5

   ....37.5 litres.......... 1 mark

   b) The capacity of her car's petrol tank is 50 litres. How many more litres of petrol would she need to buy to fill the tank?

   Subtract the volume of petrol she has now from the volume of petrol she would have if the tank was full.

   .... 1 mark

2. Jessie buys a 500 ml bottle of cordial. Every day she drinks 10 ml of cordial. How many days does the bottle of cordial last?

   .... 2 marks

   1 litre = 1,000 ml

3. Here are two recipes for ice cream.

Raspberry ice cream	Chocolate ice cream
600 ml cream	1 litre of cream
1 kg raspberries	4 eggs
250 g sugar	100 g chocolate

   a) Joy has 750 ml of cream. She says she has enough cream to make the chocolate ice-cream recipe. Is she right? Explain how you know.

   ....

   .... 1 mark

   b) Joy decides to make the raspberry ice cream. How much cream does she have left after she has made the ice cream?

   .... 1 mark

3

Had a go ☐   Nearly there ☐   Nailed it! ☐   **Measures**

Reading scales

1. Read each scale and write the amount shown.

   First find out what each interval is worth. Make sure you count the gaps and not the lines.

   a) 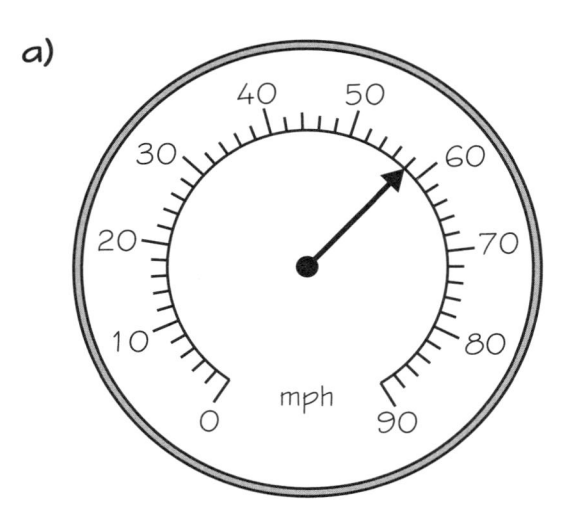

   ....58 mph.......... 1 mark

   b) 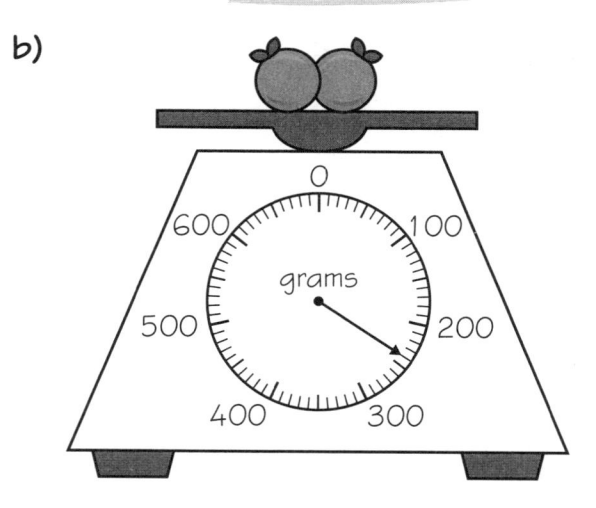

   .... grams   1 mark

   c) 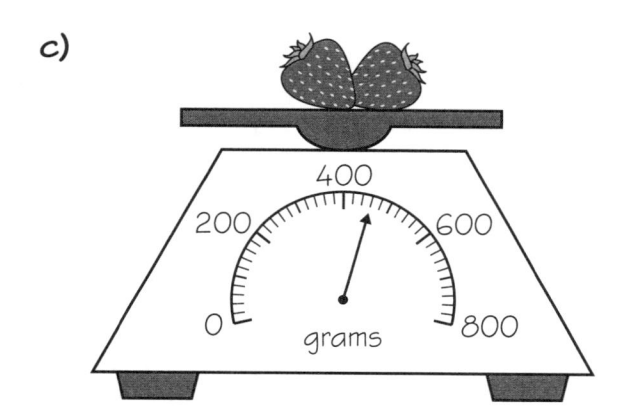

   .... grams   1 mark

   d) 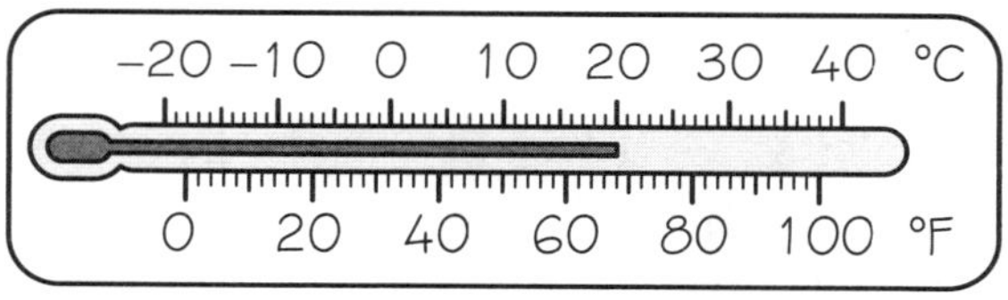

   .... °F   1 mark

2. Look carefully at these two jugs.
   Which jug contains more liquid?
   Explain how you know.

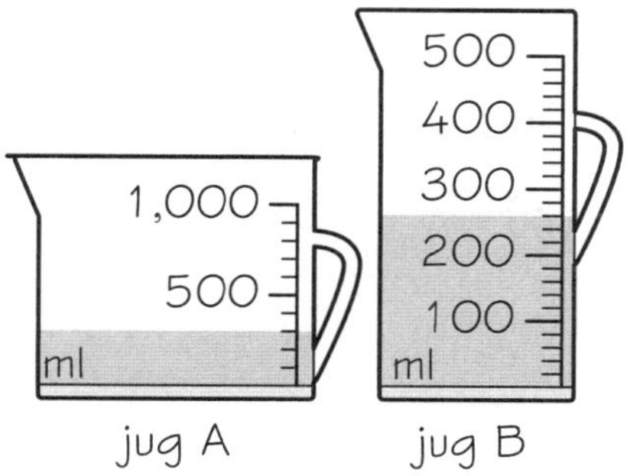

   ....

   ....   2 marks

4

Measures — Had a go ☐   Nearly there ☐   Nailed it! ☐

Converting units

1. Convert these measurements into the units asked for. One has been done for you.

   Read the units carefully and think about which units you need to convert to.

   a) 1.6 cm in millimetres

   1.6 × 10 = 16

   ....16 mm.......   1 mark

   b) 132 cm in millimetres

   ....   1 mark

   c) 3,684 cm in metres

   ....   1 mark

   d) 8,572 cm in metres

   ....   1 mark

   e) 6,734 ml in litres

   ....   1 mark

   f) 8,243 ml in litres

   ....   1 mark

2. Zoe weighs some nectarines. The scale shows 6.25 kg. What is this in grams?

   ....   1 mark

3. A bucket holds 5.275 litres of water. Alfie pours 830 ml water from the bucket into his empty fish tank. How much water is still in the bucket?

   ....   1 mark

4. Boyd is mixing plaster. He needs 600 g of powder and 330 ml of water.

   a) He takes the powder from a 2 kg packet. How much powder is left in the packet in grams?

   ....   1 mark

   b) He takes the water from a half-litre bottle. How much water is left in the bottle in millilitres?

   ....   1 mark

Had a go ☐   Nearly there ☐   Nailed it! ☐   **Measures**

Ordering measures

1. Put these lengths in order of size, starting with the smallest.

   2.5 m   168 mm   18 m   56 cm   11 km   5 cm

   ....

   .... 2 marks

2. Put these capacities in order of size, starting with the smallest.

   930 ml   13 litres   672 ml $\frac{3}{4}$ litres   482 ml $\frac{4}{5}$ litres

   ....

   .... 2 marks

3. Put these weights in order of size, starting with the smallest.

   4 kg   44 kg   300 g   16 kg   2,500 g   3 kg

   ....

   .... 2 marks

4. Look at each of these comparisons. Are they true or false?
   Circle your answer.

   a) 3,200 mm is longer than 32 cm.   true   false   1 mark

   b) 5,300 g is heavier than 514 kg.   true   false   1 mark

   c) 25 litres is a smaller capacity than 600 ml.   true   false   1 mark

5. Look at each of these comparisons.   *< means 'is less than' and*
   Insert < or > between the measures.   *> means 'is more than'.*

   a) 300 cm   ......<......   30 m   1 mark

   b) 7,000 g   ....   75 kg   1 mark

   c) 600 ml   ....   0.06 litres 1 mark

6

Measures | Had a go ☐ | Nearly there ☐ | Nailed it! ☐

Calculating with measures

1. Nastassia weighs four booklets. Each weighs 0.27 kg.

   > Make sure all measurements are in the same units before you calculate.

   a) What is the weight of one booklet in grams?

   0.27 kg × 1,000 = 270 g .... **1 mark**

   b) What is the total weight of the four booklets in grams?

   .... **1 mark**

   c) What is the total weight of the four booklets in kilograms?

   .... **1 mark**

2. Find the sum of 3.325 litres and 246 millilitres. Give your answer in litres.

   ....
   .... **1 mark**

3. Rebecca jumps 1.3 m. What is the length of eight of her jumps in metres?

   ....
   .... **1 mark**

4. Dr Clint went on a sailing holiday. She sailed 43 km on the first day, and 56.7 km on the second. She wants to cover 150 km in three days. How far does she need to sail on the third day?

   ....
   .... **2 marks**

5. Mark is baking a sponge cake. He starts by adding 720 g of sugar to 0.68 kg of butter. What is the total weight of his mixture in grams?

   ....
   .... **2 marks**

Had a go ☐ Nearly there ☐ Nailed it! ☐

Measures

Imperial units

1. 1 inch is approximately 2.5 cm.

   a) Approximately how many centimetres are there in 40 inches?

   40 × 2.5 = 100

   ....100 cm....... 1 mark

   b) Approximately how many inches are there in 160 cm?

   .... 1 mark

2. 1 pound is approximately 450 g.

   a) Approximately how many grams are there in 30 pounds?

   .... 1 mark

   b) Approximately how many pounds are there in 9,000 g?

   .... 1 mark

3. 1 pint is approximately 500 ml.

   Approximately how many millilitres are there in 4.5 pints?

   .... 1 mark

4. 1 mile is approximately 1.6 km. Tina's friend Angela is visiting from Germany, where distances are given in kilometres.

	Sheffield	Leeds	London
Sheffield		35	167
Leeds	35		195
London	167	195	

   Angela wants to know the distances between some cities in the UK. Here is a table of distances in miles.

   a) How far is it from Sheffield to Leeds in kilometres?

   .... 2 marks

   b) How far is a round trip from Leeds to London in kilometres?

   A round trip means travelling there and back.

   .... 2 marks

Measures Had a go ☐ Nearly there ☐ Nailed it! ☐

Time

1. Riki caught a train at 09:50 and arrived in London at 13:05

   a) Write the time Riki caught the train in words.

   ten minutes to ten in the morning .... 1 mark

   b) Write the time he arrived in London in words.

   > 13:05 is in the afternoon. Take 12 off the hours to find the time in 12-hour clock.

   .... 1 mark

2. Gemma's plane left the UK at 22:30. It was due to arrive in Spain at 01:40

   a) Write the time Gemma's plane left the UK in words.

   .... 1 mark

   b) Gemma's plane was 15 minutes late arriving in Spain. Write the time that Gemma's plane arrived in Spain in words.

   .... 1 mark

3. This timetable shows the times of trains between Dore and Edale on a Sunday.

Dore	09:22	10:27	11:43	12:35	14:18
Hope	09:39	10:44	12:00	12:52	14:35
Edale	09:48	10:53	12:09	13:01	14:44

   a) How long is there between the first two trains from Dore?

   .... hours and .... minutes   1 mark

   b) How long is the journey from Dore to Edale?

   .... 1 mark

   c) How long is the journey from Hope to Edale?

   .... 1 mark

Had a go ☐   Nearly there ☐   Nailed it! ☐   **Measures**

Money

1. Rosie is doing a sponsored silence for one hour. Calculate how much each person promises in pounds. One has been done for you.

   a) Chris promises 5p a minute.

   5p × 60 = £3 .... 1 mark

   b) Sara promises 15p a minute.

   .... 1 mark

   c) Amy promises 8p a minute.

   .... 1 mark

2. A shop sells bookmarks and stickers.

   a) Tara buys three bookmarks. How much does she pay in pounds?

   Bookmarks: 45p each

   Stickers: small pack 15p large pack 25p

   .... 1 mark

   b) Adil buys a bookmark and two small packs of stickers. How much does he pay?

   .... 2 marks

   c) Bronwyn buys eight bookmarks and pays with a £5 note. How much change does she get?

   .... 2 marks

   d) How many large packs of stickers can Oliver buy for £5?

   .... 2 marks

10

Measures Had a go ☐   Nearly there ☐   Nailed it! ☐

Perimeter and area

1. Calculate the perimeters and areas of these shapes.

   a) 5 cm / 2 cm rectangle

   perimeter = 2 cm + 5 cm + 2 cm + 5 cm

   perimeter = 14 cm

   area = 2 cm × 5 cm

   area = 10 cm²

   2 marks

   b) 4 cm / 3 cm rectangle

   perimeter = ...

   area = ...

   2 marks

2. This shape has an area of 6 cm².
   Find its perimeter.

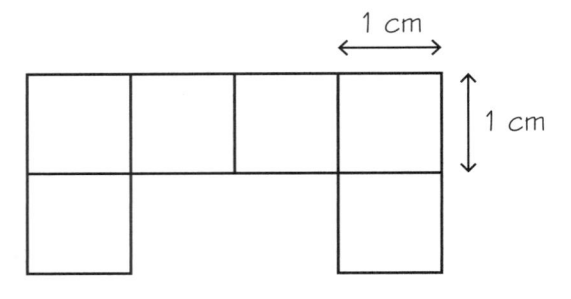

   1 cm
   1 cm

   Not to scale

   > Perimeter is measured in units of length (like cm). Area is measured in square units (like cm²).

   .... 1 mark

3. A rectangle has an area of 6 cm² and a perimeter of 10 cm. What are its dimensions?

   .... × .... 1 mark

4. This hexagon has been drawn on centimetre-squared paper.
   Explain how you know the perimeter is greater than 6 cm.

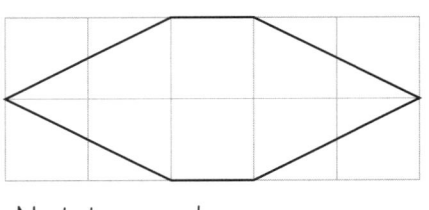

   Not to scale

   ....
   ....
   ....
   ....
   1 mark

Had a go ☐   Nearly there ☐   Nailed it! ☐   **Measures**

Compound shapes

1. Calculate the perimeters and areas of these compound shapes.

   Split each shape into rectangles. Add their areas to find the total area.

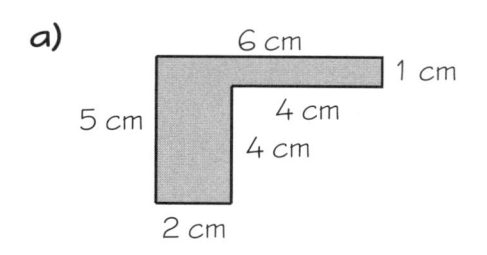

   a) [shape with labels: 6 cm, 1 cm, 5 cm, 4 cm, 4 cm, 2 cm]

   perimeter = 2 + 5 + 6 + 1 + 4 + 4

   = 22

   area = (2 × 4) + (6 × 1)

   = 14

   perimeter = ...22 cm...   area = ...14 cm²...

   2 marks

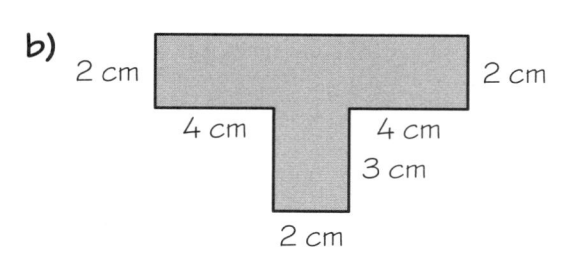

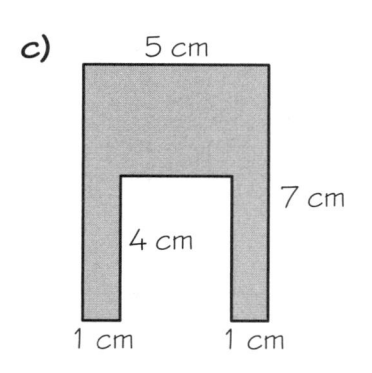

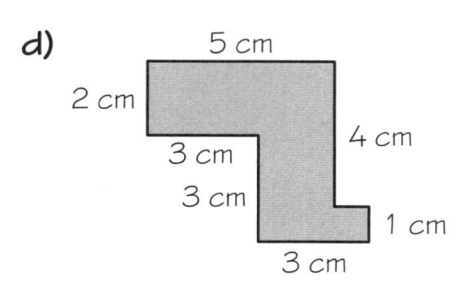

   b) [shape with labels: 2 cm, 2 cm, 4 cm, 4 cm, 3 cm, 2 cm]

   perimeter = ...   area = ...

   2 marks

   c) [shape with labels: 5 cm, 7 cm, 4 cm, 1 cm, 1 cm]

   perimeter = ...   area = ...

   2 marks

   d) [shape with labels: 5 cm, 2 cm, 3 cm, 4 cm, 3 cm, 1 cm, 3 cm]

   perimeter = ...   area = ...

   2 marks

12

Measures | Had a go ☐ Nearly there ☐ Nailed it! ☐

Areas of triangles

1. Calculate the areas of these triangles.

area of a triangle = $\frac{1}{2}$ base × height

a)

6 cm
5 cm

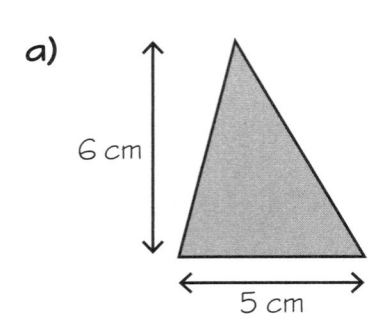

area = $\frac{1}{2}$ × 5 × 6

= $\frac{1}{2}$ (5 × 6)

= $\frac{1}{2}$ × 30

= 15

area = ...15 cm²...   2 marks

b)

4 cm
3 cm

area = ...   2 marks

2. This diagram shows three triangles.

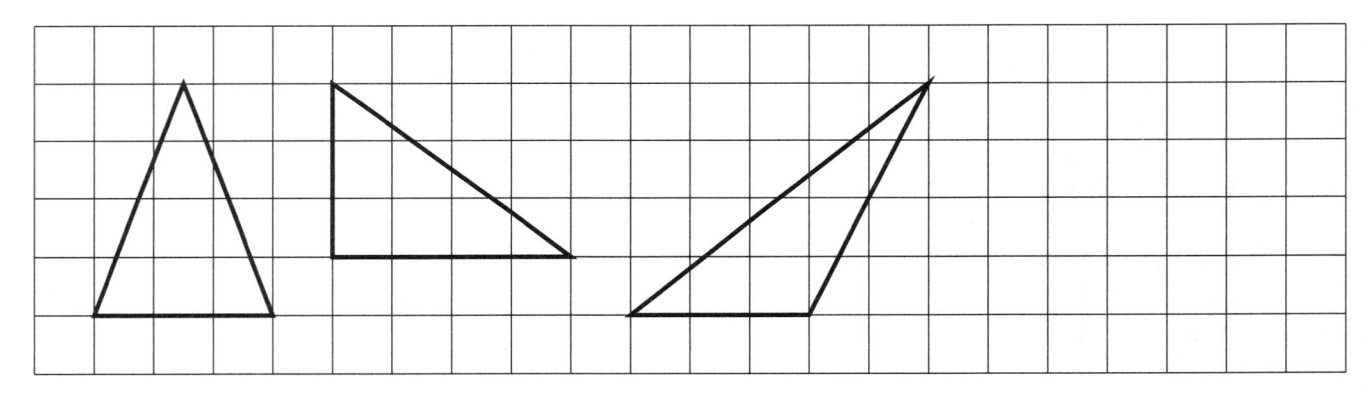

a) Sophia says that all three triangles have the same area.

Is she correct? Explain how you know.

....

....   2 marks

b) On the grid, draw another triangle that has the same area.   2 marks

13

Had a go ☐   Nearly there ☐   Nailed it! ☐   **Measures**

Areas of parallelograms

1. Calculate the areas of these parallelograms.

   area of a parallelogram = base length × height

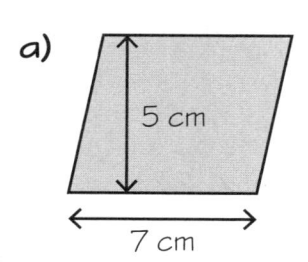

   a) [5 cm height, 7 cm base]

   area = 5 cm × 7 cm

   area = 35 cm² ....   2 marks

   b) [7 cm height, 8 cm base]

   area = ...   2 marks

2. Each square on this grid represents 1 cm. Which of the following shapes have an area of 6 cm²?

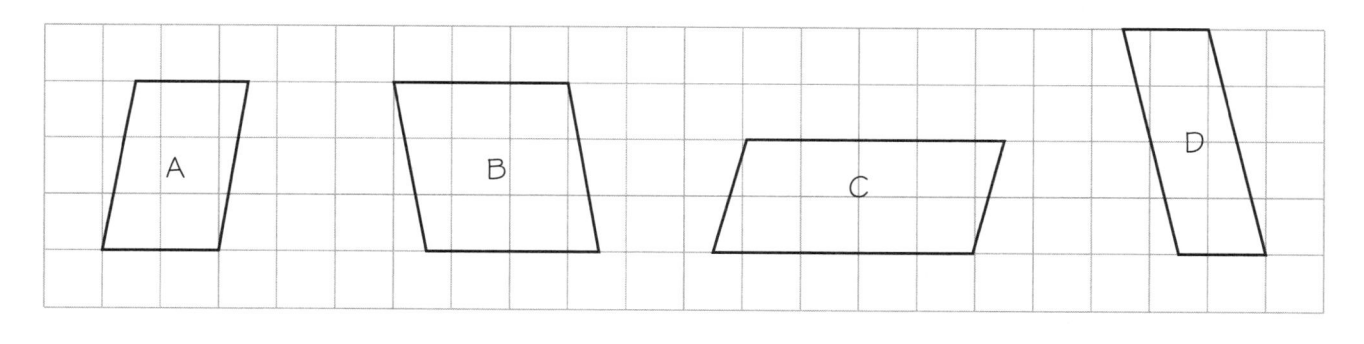

   [Grid with shapes A, B, C, D]

   ....   2 marks

3. Kaspar says he has drawn a parallelogram with an area of 8 cm².
   Lydia says that the perimeter must be shorter than 8 cm. Is Lydia correct?
   Explain your answer.

   ....

   ....   2 marks

14

| Measures | Had a go ☐ | Nearly there ☐ | Nailed it! ☐ |

Volumes of cuboids

1. Calculate the volumes of these cuboids. One has been done for you.

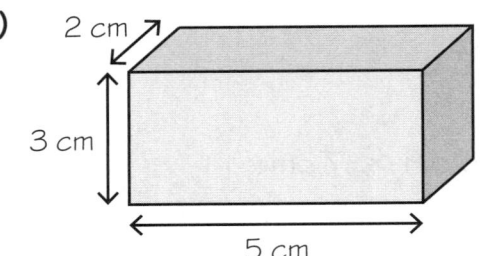

   > volume of a cuboid = length × width × height
   > Don't forget the answer needs to be in cubed units.

   a) 2 cm, 3 cm, 5 cm

   volume = 5 cm × 3 cm × 2 cm

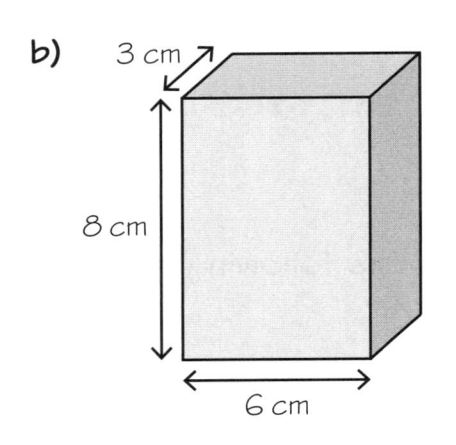

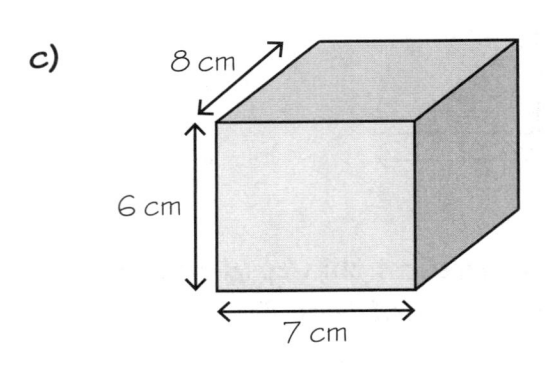

   volume = 30 cm³ .... 2 marks

   b) 3 cm, 8 cm, 6 cm

   volume = ... 2 marks

   c) 8 cm, 6 cm, 7 cm

   volume = ... 2 marks

2. A swimming pool is 3 m deep, 10 m long and 6 m wide. What is its volume?

   .... 1 mark

3. A cuboid has a base area of 8 cm². It has a volume of 24 cm³. What is its height?

   .... 2 marks

4. A cuboid has a volume of 27 cm³. Olly says this shape is a cube.

   Which of the following statements is true? Explain your answer.

   A He is definitely correct.   B He could be correct.   C He is definitely not correct.

   ....

   .... 1 mark

15

Had a go ☐   Nearly there ☐   Nailed it! ☐   **Geometry**

Triangles and quadrilaterals

1. Here are five shapes. Which two fit together to make a square?

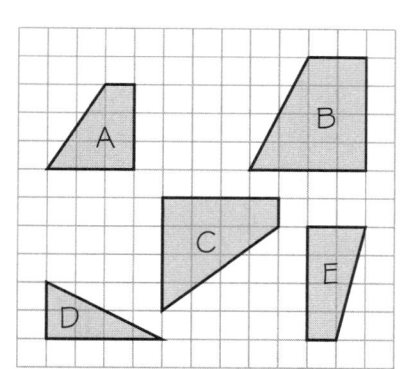

   > You might need to rotate the shapes. You could use tracing paper to help.

   .... and .... 1 mark

2. Here are six quadrilaterals. Alison chooses one of the quadrilaterals.

   She says, 'All sides are the same length. The shape has two acute angles.'

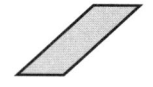

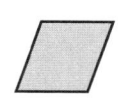

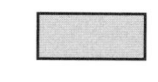

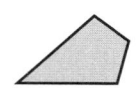

   square   parallelogram   rhombus   rectangle   kite   trapezium

   Which shape did Alison choose?

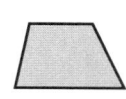

   .... 1 mark

3. Clint has three small equilateral triangles and one large equilateral triangle. The small equilateral triangles have sides of 8 cm. Clint makes this shape.

   Calculate the perimeter of Clint's shape.

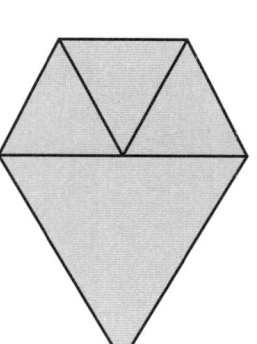

   > The perimeter is the distance around the edge of a shape.

   .... 2 marks

16

Geometry

Had a go ☐   Nearly there ☐   Nailed it! ☐

Circles

1. Aisha draws this logo.

   It has a straight side and two equal semi-circles.

   Each semi-circle has an area of 15 cm².

   What is the total area of the logo?

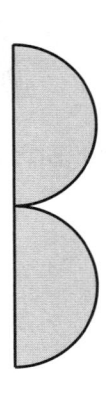

   .... 1 mark

2. Two identical small circles fit exactly inside one larger circle. The diameter of the large circle is 18 cm. What is the radius of one small circle?

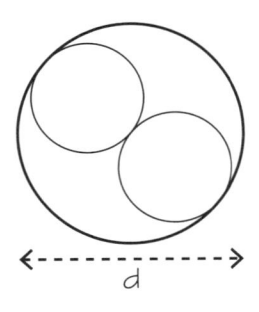

   .... 1 mark

3. Jerry cuts a circle into quarters and arranges the pieces in this pattern. What is the total length of the pattern she creates?

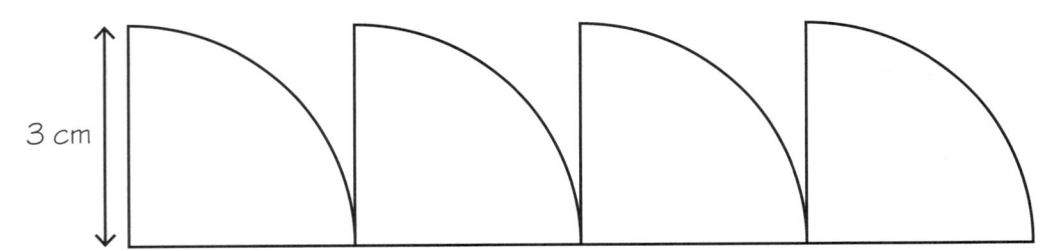

   3 cm

   .... 1 mark

Had a go ☐   Nearly there ☐   Nailed it! ☐   **Geometry**

Other 2D shapes

1. Look at these shapes and complete the sentences below. One has been done for you.

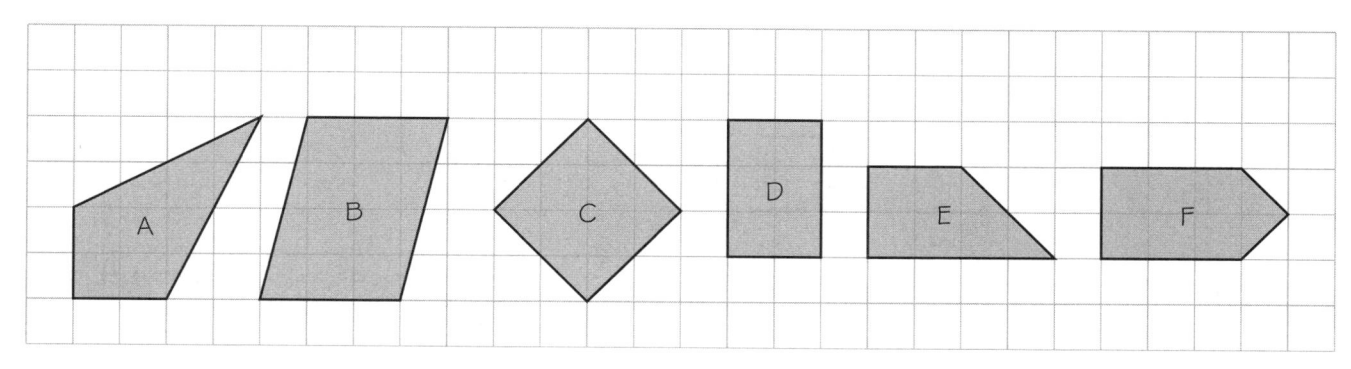

   a) Shape ....A........ is a kite.

   b) Shape .... is not a quadrilateral.

   c) Shape .... has only two right angles.

   d) Shape .... has two acute angles.   **4 marks**

2. Here are five shapes on a grid. Write in the missing letters below.

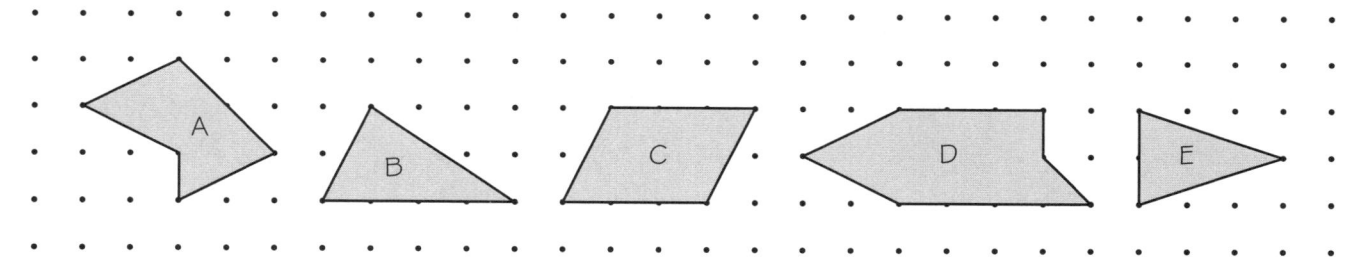

   a) Shape .... has two pairs of parallel sides.

   b) Shape .... is a pentagon.

   c) Shape .... has reflective symmetry.   **3 marks**

Geometry

Had a go ☐   Nearly there ☐   Nailed it! ☐

Properties of 2D shapes

1. Here are two shapes made from centimetre squares.

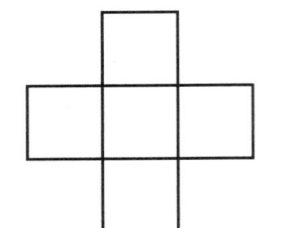

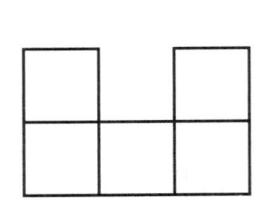

   area = space inside a shape
   perimeter = distance around the edge of a shape

   Cross out one word in each sentence to make the sentences correct.

   a) The perimeters of the shapes are *the same / different*.   **1 mark**

   b) The areas of the shapes are *the same / different*.   **1 mark**

2. The area of a rectangle is 16 cm². One of the sides is 2 cm long. What is the perimeter of the rectangle?

   .... **1 mark**

3. On the shapes below, join three dots to make:

   a) an equilateral triangle

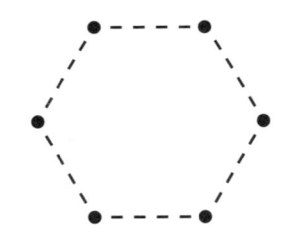

   b) an isosceles triangle.

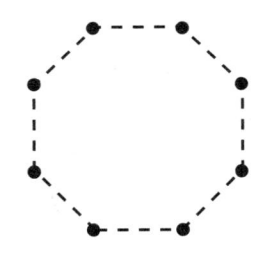

   1 mark   **1 mark**

4. Here are five shapes. Which is a rhombus?

   shape ....

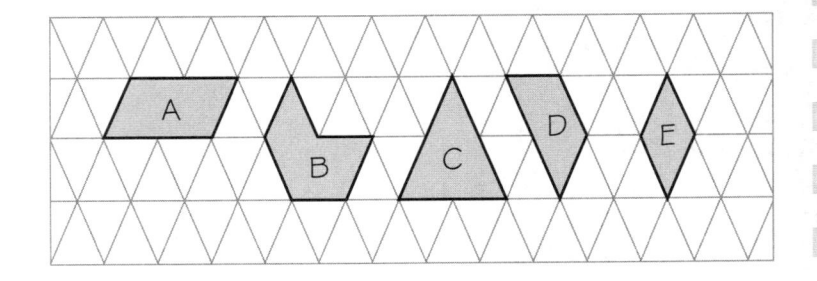

   1 mark

Had a go ☐   Nearly there ☐   Nailed it! ☐   **Geometry**

Drawing 2D shapes

1. Draw two straight lines on this shape from point A to divide it into a square and two triangles.

   Draw your lines carefully with a ruler and a sharp pencil.

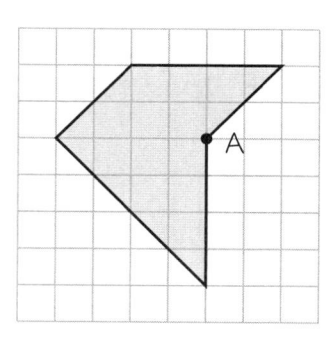

   2 marks

2. On this grid, join three dots to make a triangle that does not have a right angle.

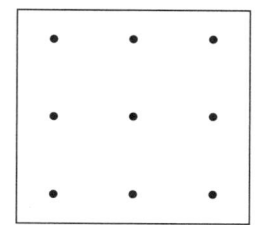

   2 marks

3. Draw two more straight lines on this grid to make a rectangle.

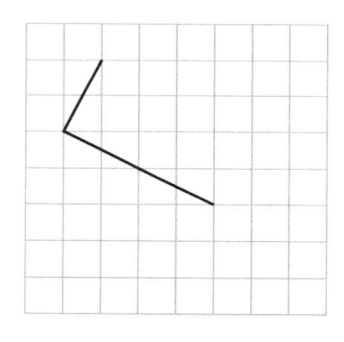

   2 marks

4. The line on this grid is one side of a square. Draw three more lines to make the other sides of the square.

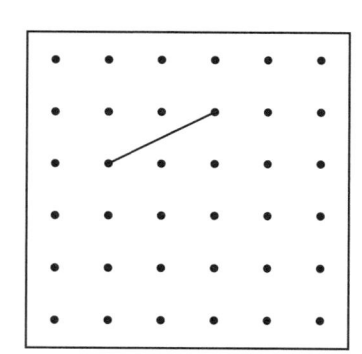

   2 marks

20

Geometry — Had a go ☐   Nearly there ☐   Nailed it! ☐

Naming 3D shapes

1. Draw arrows to match each shape to its mathematical name. One has been done for you.

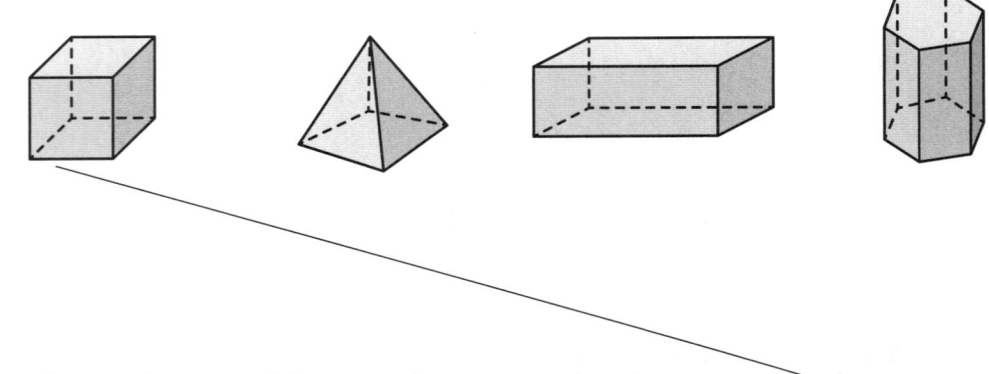

   square-based pyramid   hexagonal prism   cube   cuboid

   3 marks

2. Write the mathematical name for these 3D shapes.

   a) 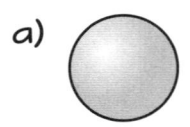 ....   **1 mark**

   b) 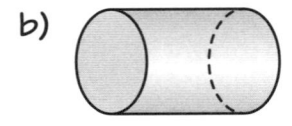 ....   **1 mark**

   c) 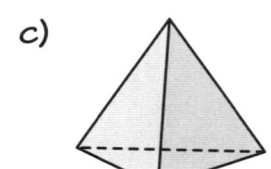 ....   **1 mark**

3. Kathy thinks of a 3D shape. She says, 'It has five faces. The two opposite faces are triangles. The other faces are rectangles.'
   What is the name of Kathy's 3D shape?

   ....   **1 mark**

21

Had a go ☐   Nearly there ☐   Nailed it! ☐   **Geometry**

Nets

1. Look at each of these nets. Put a tick in the box below the ones that fold to make a square-based pyramid.

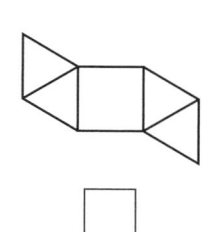

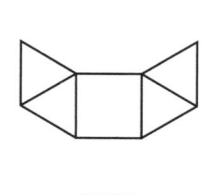

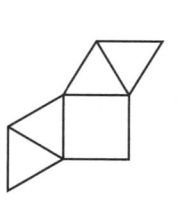

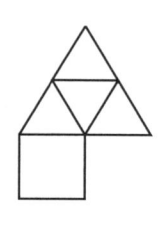

   ☐   ☐   ☐   ☐

   2 marks

2. The diagram shows an open top cube and its net. On the net, put a tick on the square which shows the base of the cube.

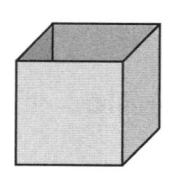

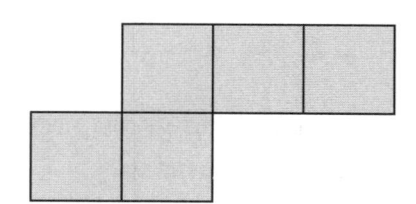

   1 mark

3. This is a pentagonal prism.

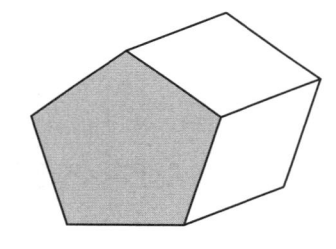

   A prism has a pair of faces that are the same shape.

   Tick the net that folds to make the pentagonal prism.

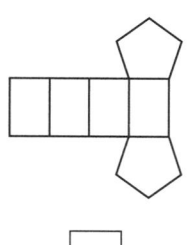

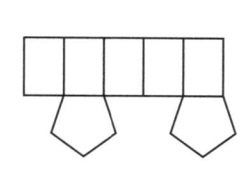

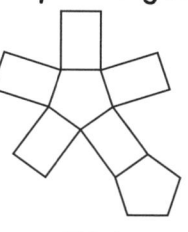

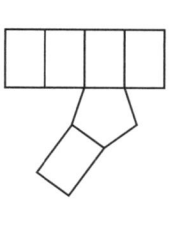

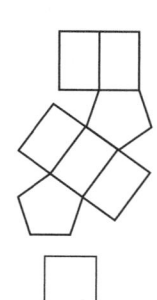

   ☐   ☐   ☐   ☐   ☐

   1 mark

4. The top half of the cube is shaded grey.

   Complete the shading on the net to match the cube.

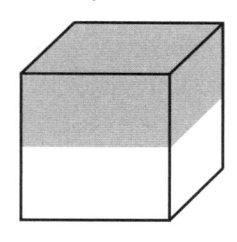

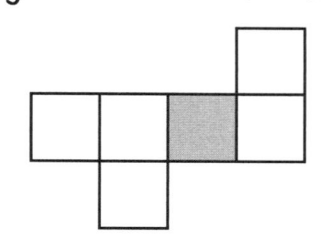

   2 marks

22

| Geometry | Had a go ☐ | Nearly there ☐ | Nailed it! ☐ |

Angles

1. Here are four shapes. Each shape has a different number of right angles.

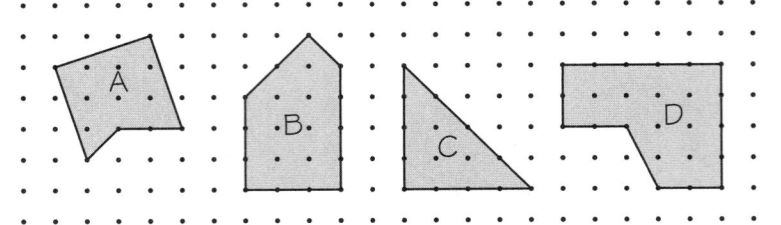

   List the shapes in order of their number of right angles, starting with the shape that has the fewest.

   .... 1 mark

2. In this diagram, four angles are labelled a, b, c and d.

   Write the letters of the angles that are obtuse.

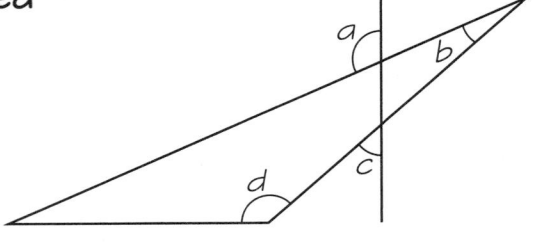

   .... 1 mark

3. Here are five triangles. Write the letter of each triangle that has a right angle.

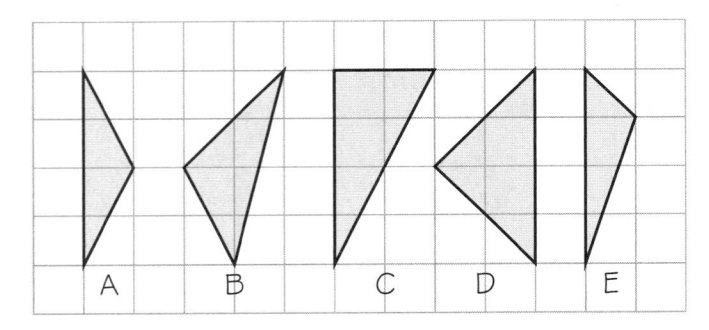

   .... 1 mark

4. Look at this shape.

   Draw a tick next to the angles which are smaller than a right angle.

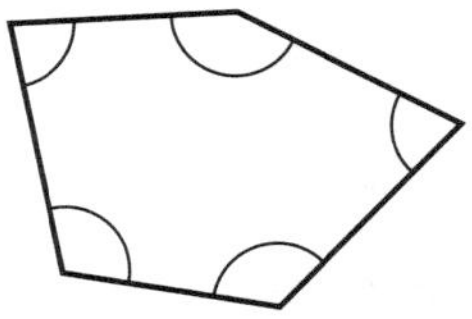

   1 mark

5. Khaled draws a triangle. He says, 'Two of the three angles in my triangle are obtuse.' Explain why he cannot be correct.

   > An obtuse angle is more than 90 degrees but less than 180 degrees.

   ....

   .... 2 marks

| Had a go ☐ | Nearly there ☐ | Nailed it! ☐ | **Geometry** |

Measuring angles

1. Measure these angles accurately. State whether each angle is acute, obtuse or reflex.

   A reflex angle is greater than 180 degrees.

   a)

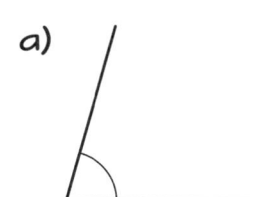

   .... 75°, acute .... 1 mark

   b)

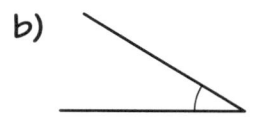

   .... 1 mark

   c)

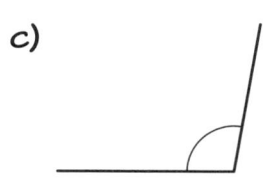

   .... 1 mark

   d)

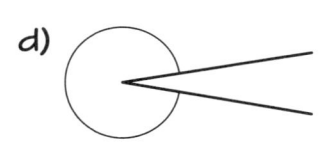

   .... 1 mark

2. This pie chart shows the favourite animals of a class. Measure all four angles in the pie chart.

   Estimate each angle by eye. Then measure accurately with a protractor.

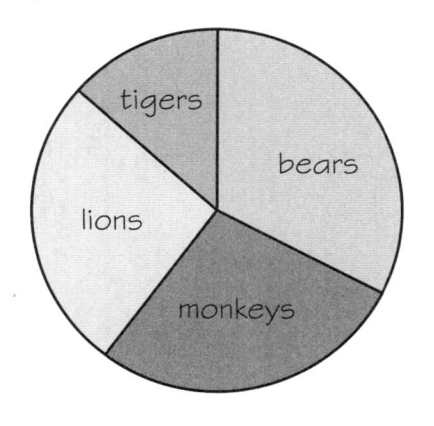

   lions   .... 1 mark

   tigers   .... 1 mark

   bears   .... 1 mark

   monkeys   .... 1 mark

24

Geometry

Had a go ☐   Nearly there ☐   Nailed it! ☐

Finding unknown angles

1. This is a diagram of three quarters of a car wheel.

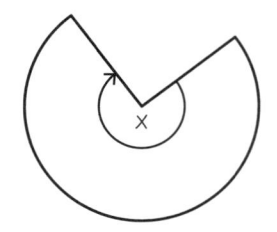

   x

   Not to scale

   How many degrees is angle x?

   Angles around a point always add up to 360 degrees, so you need to work out three quarters of 360

   .... 1 mark

2. Here is an isosceles triangle.

   Calculate the size of angle y.

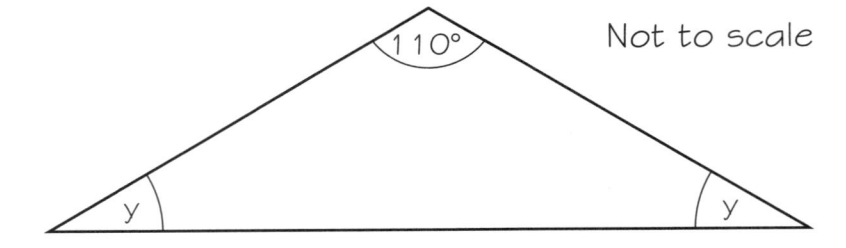

   110°   Not to scale
   y y

   .... 1 mark

3. Calculate the size of angle z in this diagram.

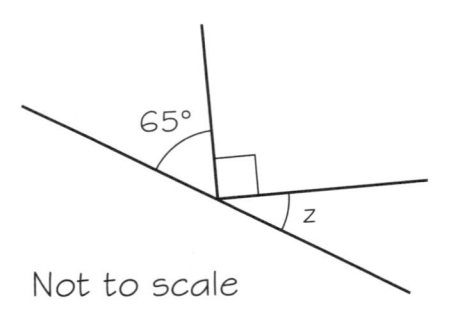

   65°
   z

   Not to scale

   .... 1 mark

4. Look at this diagram.

   Calculate the sizes of angles a and b.

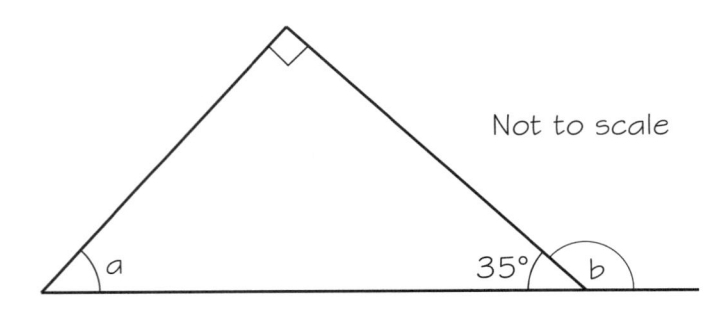

   Not to scale

   a 35° b

   a = ...

   b = ...   1 mark

25

Had a go ☐   Nearly there ☐   Nailed it! ☐   **Geometry**

Coordinates

1. A, B and C are three corners of a square.

   What are the coordinates of the other corner?

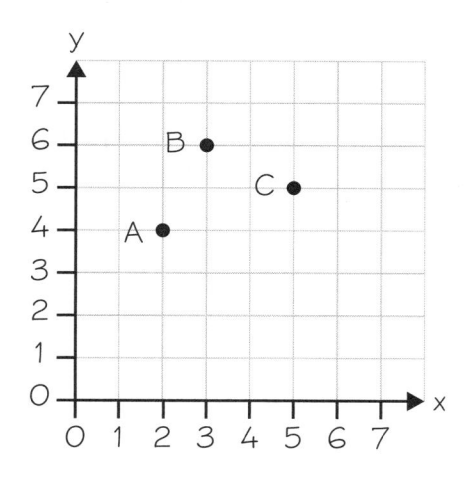

   ....   **2 marks**

2. Here is one side of a square drawn on a coordinate grid. The square has a vertex at (6, 1). Draw the other three sides of the square.

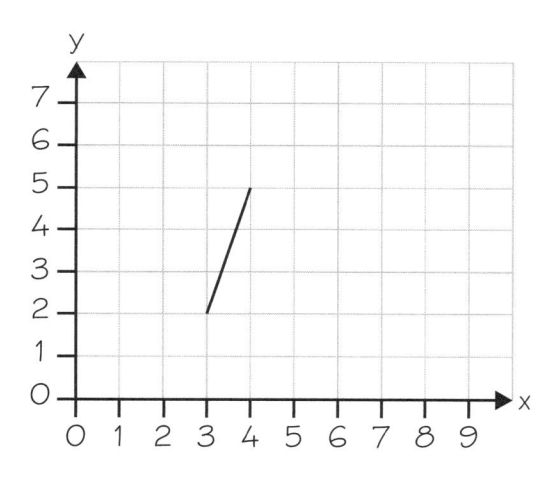

   > Mark the values of each vertex on the grid to help you.

   1 mark

3. Here is a right-angled triangle drawn on a coordinate grid.

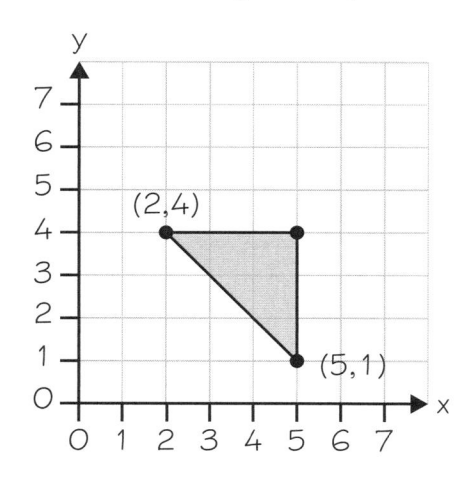

   Write the coordinates of the unlabelled vertex.   ....   **2 marks**

26

| Geometry | Had a go ☐ | Nearly there ☐ | Nailed it! ☐ |

Translation

> When you translate an object, you can 'slide' it in any direction. The shape does not rotate.

1. a) Translate this shape 7 squares right and 6 squares down.

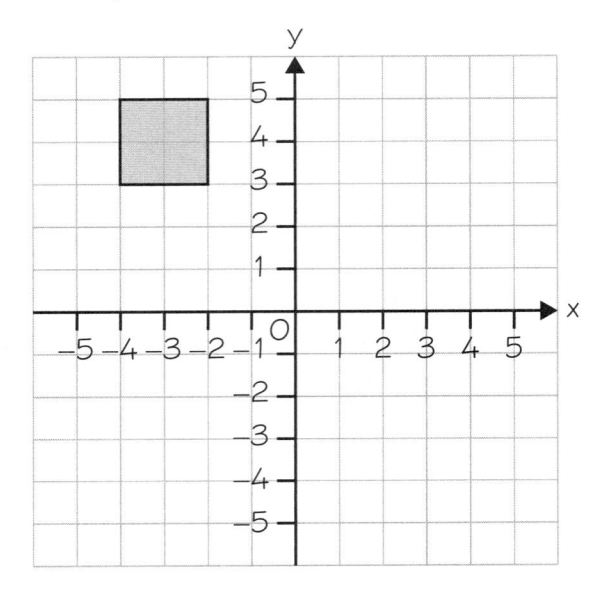

   b) Translate this shape 5 squares left and 4 squares down.

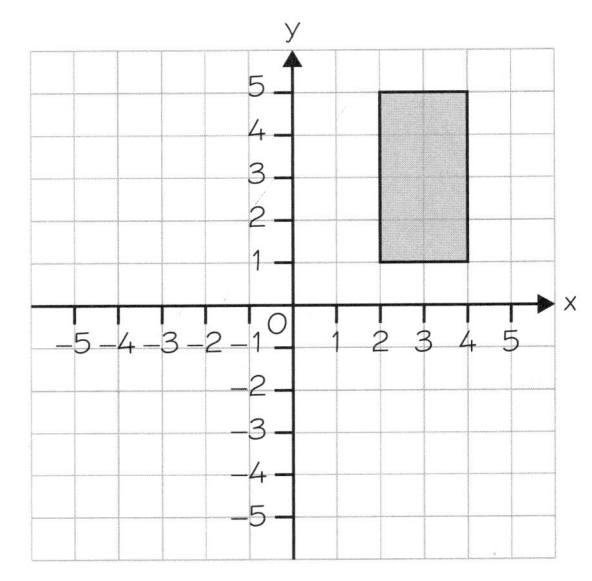

   1 mark   1 mark

2. For each grid, describe how shape A is translated to get shape B.

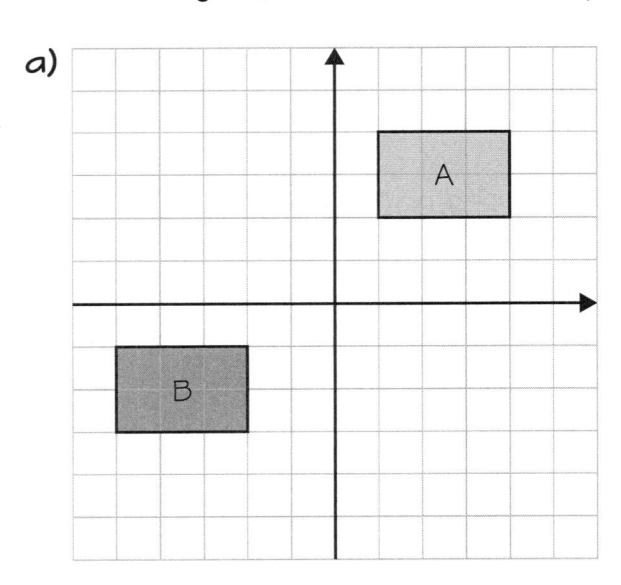

   a) five squares down and

   six squares left   1 mark

   b) ....

   ....   1 mark

27

| Had a go ☐ | Nearly there ☐ | Nailed it! ☐ | **Geometry** |

Reflection

1. Draw two more circles on this grid to make a design that has a line of symmetry.

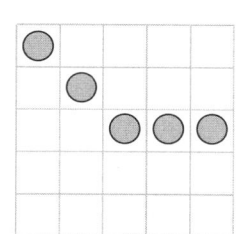

   1 mark

2. Here are five patterns. Put a tick or a cross in each box to show whether the pattern has a line of symmetry.

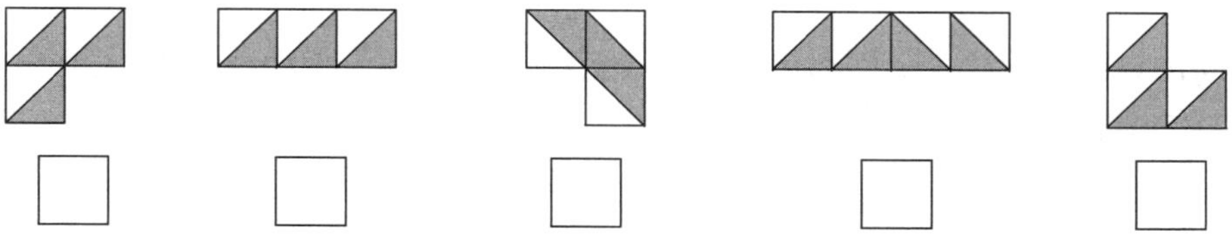

   ☐   ☐   ☐   ☐   ☐

   1 mark

3. Reflect these shapes in the mirror lines shown.

   a)

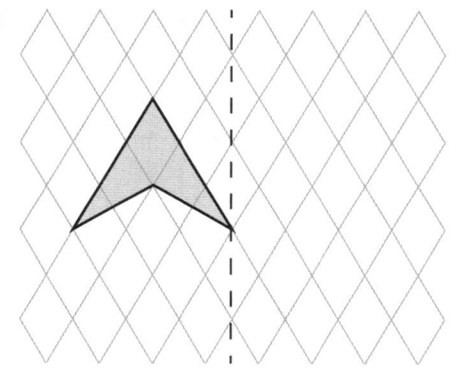

   b)

   1 mark   **1 mark**

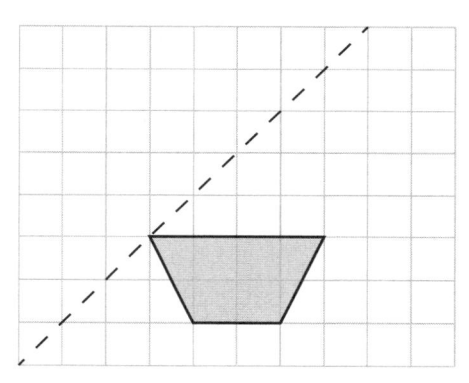

4. Reflect this shape in the y-axis.

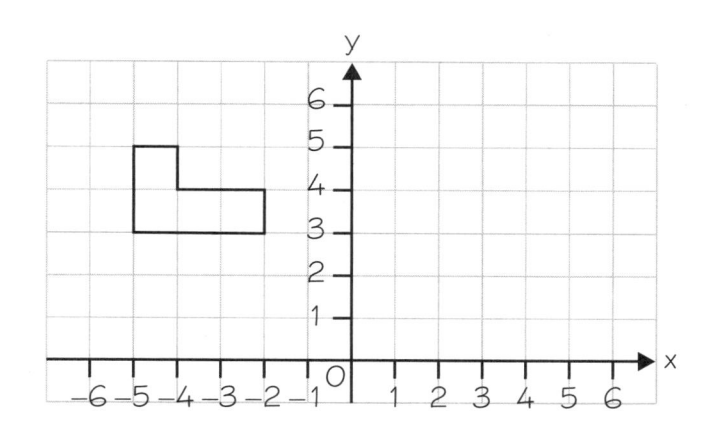

   2 marks

28

Statistics — Had a go ☐ Nearly there ☐ Nailed it! ☐

Tables

1. This table shows the heights and dates of birth of four children in a school.

name	height	date of birth
Theo	1 m 19 cm	30 September 2002
Daisy	1 m 15 cm	15 July 2005
Tariq	1 m 23 cm	7 May 2004
Chloe	1 m 11 cm	18 October 2007

   a) Who is the tallest?

   ......Tariq...... **1 mark**

   b) Who is the oldest?

   .... **1 mark**

   c) How much taller is Theo than Chloe? .... **1 mark**

2. This table shows what five children had for their school lunch.

	chips	jacket potato	cheese flan	fish	vegetable flan
Ophelia		✓		✓	
Usy	✓		✓		✓
Ramona		✓	✓		
Chris	✓			✓	
Jody		✓			✓

   a) Who had fish? .... and .... **1 mark**

   b) Who had a jacket potato as well as fish? .... **1 mark**

   c) Who had three of the options? .... **1 mark**

3. This table shows how much money some friends receive one week for doing chores.

	Fiona	Henry	Tomas	Susha
cleaning	£4.50	£5.00	£3.50	£2.75
laundry	£2.50	£3.50	£2.00	£4.25
total	£7.00	£8.50	£5.50	£7.00

   a) Who was given £3.50 for doing the laundry?

   .... **1 mark**

   b) Which two children earned the same amount of money in total?

   .... **1 mark**

Had a go ☐   Nearly there ☐   Nailed it! ☐

Statistics

Timetables

1. This is a bus timetable from Millhouses to Owlerton.

| Millhouses | 08:25 | 10:50 | 13:15 | 15:40 |
| Owlerton | 09:15 | 11:40 | 14:05 | 16:30 |

a) What time does the 10:50 bus arrive in Owlerton?

.......11:40....... **1 mark**

b) How long is the journey from Millhouses to Owlerton?

.... **1 mark**

c) Andrew is meeting Ahmed in Owlerton at half past two. What time is the latest bus he can catch from Millhouses to get there on time?

.... **1 mark**

2. This timetable shows all of the train times between Solihull and Banbury on one day.

Solihull	08:34	10:04	12:24	14:04	16:25
Warwick	08:52	10:16	12:42	14:16	16:42
Banbury	09:16	10:40	13:04	14:40	17:04

a) What is the shortest travel time between Solihull and Banbury?

.... **1 mark**

b) Callum wants to get to Banbury before five o'clock. What time is the latest train he can catch from Solihull?

.... **1 mark**

c) Trains return from Warwick to Solihull at 09:55 and every 2 hours 30 minutes after that. David takes the 10:04 train from Solihull to Warwick. He spends 4.5 hours there. What is the time of the earliest train he can get back to Solihull?

.... **2 marks**

Statistics

Had a go ☐   Nearly there ☐   Nailed it! ☐

Bar charts

1. This bar chart shows the favourite flavours of ice cream of children in a class.

   Answer the questions about the chart.

   a) Which was the most popular flavour? ....vanilla........... 1 mark

   b) How many children liked chocolate best? .... 1 mark

   c) How many more liked mint than strawberry? .... 1 mark

   d) How many children took part in the survey? .... 1 mark

2. This bar chart shows the numbers of passengers in cars passing the school entrance in one hour.

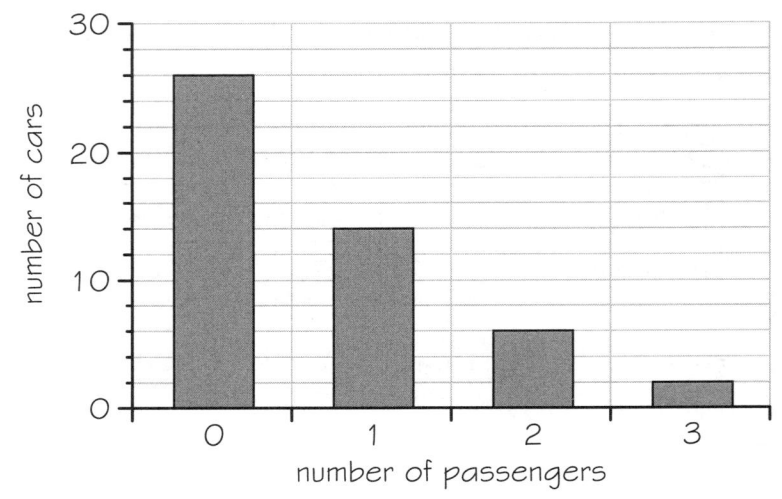

   a) How many cars with one passenger passed the school entrance during that hour?

   .... 1 mark

   b) How many cars with no passengers passed the school entrance during that hour?

   .... 1 mark

   c) How many cars in total passed the school entrance during that hour?

   .... 1 mark

Had a go ☐   Nearly there ☐   Nailed it! ☐   Statistics

Drawing bar charts

1. Draw bar charts from the following data sets.

   a) Favourite drinks of pupils in class 4B

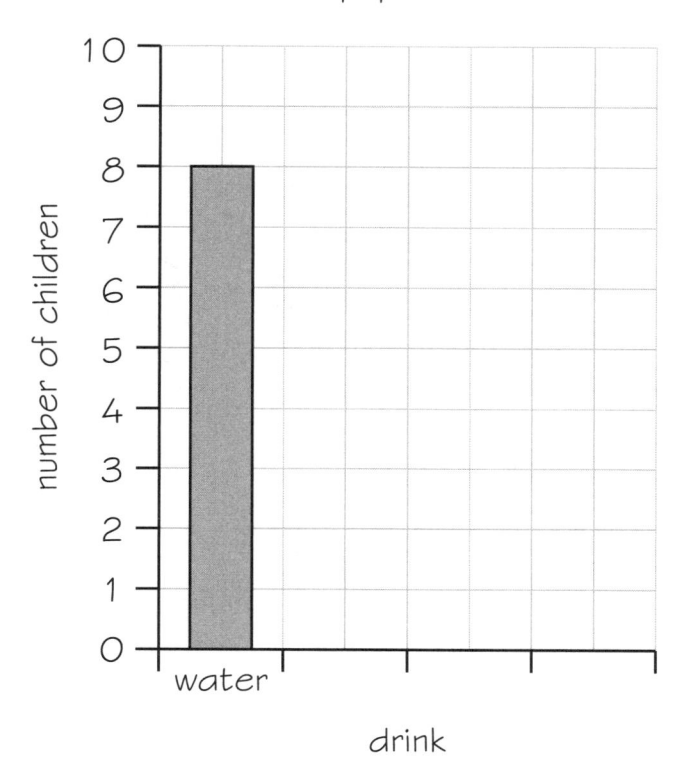

drink	children
water	8
cola	9
orange	6
lemon	3

   4 marks

   b) Favourite fruit of children at Forest Road School

fruit	children
apples	30
bananas	40
grapes	20
oranges	35
pears	10

   4 marks

32

Statistics Had a go ☐   Nearly there ☐   Nailed it! ☐

Pie charts

1. James visited his grandparents after school on 36 days one year. The pie chart shows what days of the week they were. Answer the questions about the chart.

   Measure the angles carefully.

   a) On which day did James visit his grandparents most often?

   ....Monday......... 1 mark

   b) Did James visit more often on Tuesdays or Thursdays?

   .... 1 mark

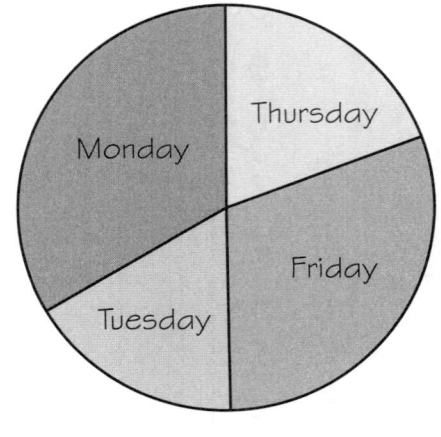

   c) James plays hockey after school on the same day each week and can't visit his grandparents that day. On which day does he play hockey?

   .... 1 mark

2. This pie chart shows the different ways in which 240 pupils came to school one day.

   a) How many pupils walked to school that day?

   .... 1 mark

   b) What fraction of the pupils came by bus?

   .... 1 mark

   c) Helen said that more people came to school by bike than by car. Is Helen correct? Give a reason for your answer.

   ....

   .... 2 marks

Had a go ☐   Nearly there ☐   Nailed it! ☐   **Statistics**

Drawing pie charts

1. Draw pie charts to show the following data.

    a) The favourite pets of children in class 4T

    9 + 15 + 6 = 30 children

    $\frac{15}{30} = \frac{1}{2}$ chose dogs. Dogs are five sectors.

    $\frac{9}{30} = \frac{3}{10}$ chose cats. Cats are three sectors.

    $\frac{6}{30} = \frac{1}{5}$ chose others. Others are two sectors.

    Each pie chart is split into ten sectors. First find out how many children are one tenth of the total.

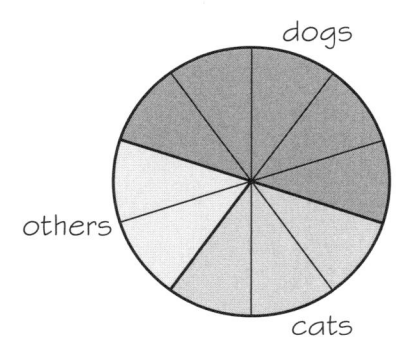

pet	children
cats	9
dogs	15
others	6

    2 marks

    b) Children's favourite flavours of crisps

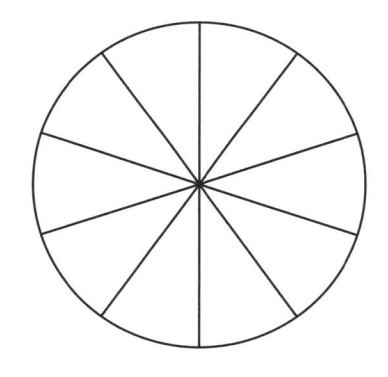

flavour	children
plain	30
salt and vinegar	40
cheese and onion	20
chicken	10

    2 marks

    c) Number of brothers and sisters of children in Pondbeck Primary School

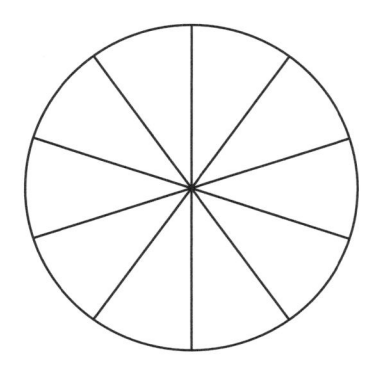

brothers or sisters	children
none	20
one	100
two	50
three	20
four	10

    2 marks

34

Statistics

Had a go ☐   Nearly there ☐   Nailed it! ☐

Line graphs

1. This line graph illustrates a marathon race that Ghalib and Sam ran.

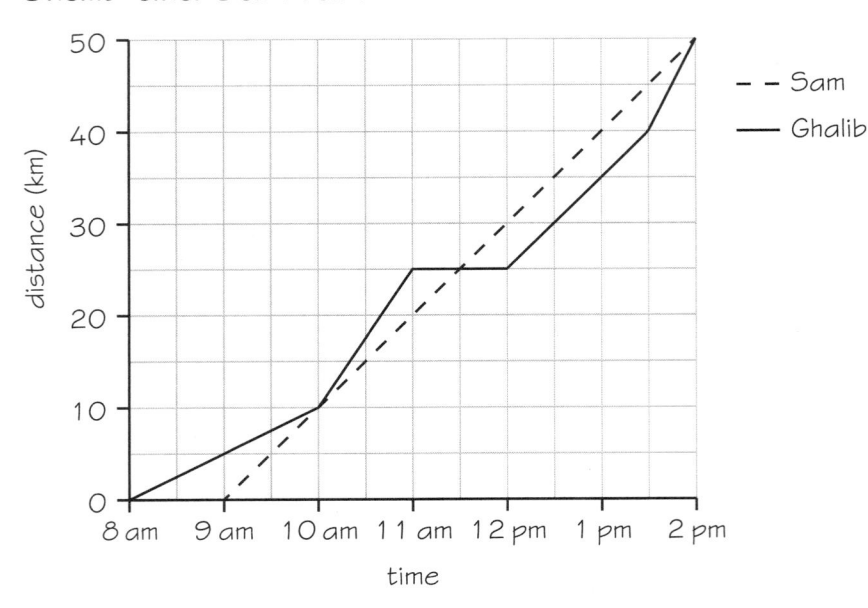

> You read the time of day on the horizontal axis and the distance run on the vertical axis.

a) What time did each athlete set off on the race?

   Ghalib.................... Sam....................   **2 marks**

b) At what time did Sam first catch up with Ghalib?

   ....   **1 mark**

c) Ghalib ran very fast to try to beat Sam, but then had to stop.

   i) How long did Ghalib stop for?   ....   **1 mark**

   ii) How far had he run by then?   ....   **1 mark**

   iii) At approximately what time did Sam pass Ghalib?

   ....   **1 mark**

d) At what point in the race did Ghalib run the fastest?

   ....   **2 marks**

e) Jenny said that the graph shows that Sam won the race. Is she correct? Explain your answer.

   ....
   ....   **1 mark**

Had a go ☐ Nearly there ☐ Nailed it! ☐   **Statistics**

Drawing line graphs

1. The temperature in Sheffield changed during one day as shown in this table.

time	06:00	08:00	10:00	12:00	14:00	16:00	18:00
temperature (°C)	0	1	3	7	8	6	2

Draw a line graph to show the data in the table.

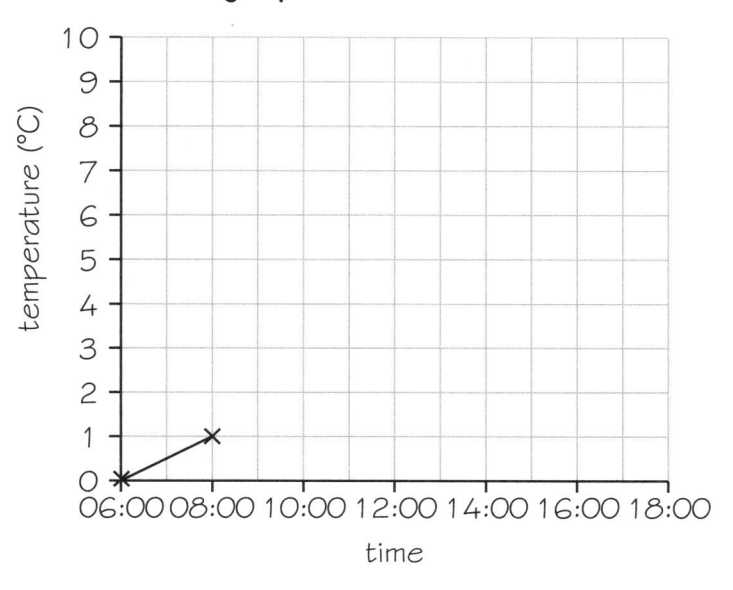

> To plot each point, go across from the vertical scale and up from the horizontal scale. Draw a cross where the two meet.

3 marks

2. This table shows how many butterflies Daniel counted in his garden one day as the temperature outside rose.

temperature (°C)	10	12	14	16	18	20	22
butterflies	0	3	5	6	12	16	20

Draw a line graph to show the data in the table.

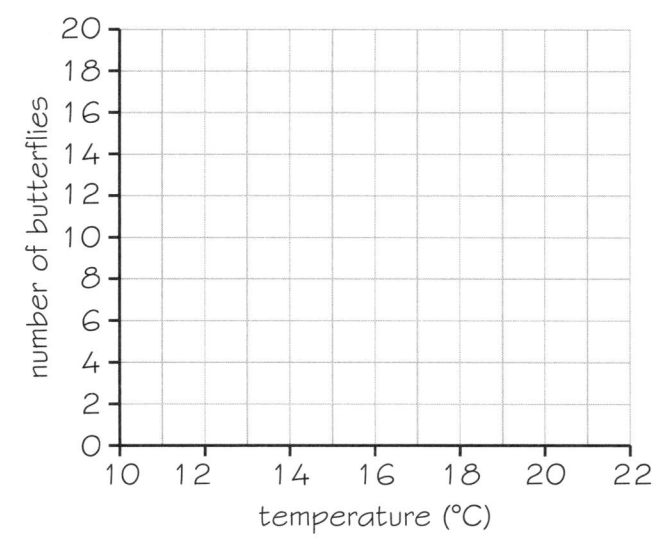

4 marks

36

Statistics — Had a go ☐ Nearly there ☐ Nailed it! ☐

Calculating the mean

1. Find the mean of the numbers in each list.

   a) £6, £8, £4, £9, £5, £10

   6 + 8 + 4 + 9 + 5 + 10 = 42

   42 ÷ 6 = 7

   To find the mean, add all the values then divide by the number of values.

   mean = ...**£7**.................... 2 marks

   b) 3 kg, 9 kg, 4 kg, 8 kg, 6 kg

   mean = ... 2 marks

   c) 19p, 28p, 41p, 32p, 58p, 9p, 38p, £1, 60p, 45p

   Make all units the same before you calculate the mean.

   mean = ... 2 marks

2. In a game, three points are given for a win, one point for a draw and no points for losing.

   a) Jess played ten games. She won two, drew four and lost the rest. What was Jess's mean score over the ten games?

   .... 2 marks

   b) John also played ten games. He had an average of two points per game. Dean said that John couldn't have lost any games at all. Is Dean correct? Explain your answer.

   ....

   ....

   2 marks

Had a go ☐ Nearly there ☐ Nailed it! ☐   **Statistics**

Using the mean

1. Navina had five maths tests one term. In the first four, she scored 44, 56, 58 and 61

   What was her score in the fifth test if she had a mean score of 60 overall?

   First find out what her total must be for all five tests.

   .... 3 marks

2. Three number cards are placed face down on a table. Two of the numbers are 4. The mean of the numbers is 5. What is the other number?

   .... 3 marks

3. The mean height of five pupils is 1.08 m.
   The heights of four of them are: 105 cm, 98 cm, 115 cm and 110 cm.
   What is the height of the fifth pupil?

   .... 3 marks

4. Four pupils have a mean of three pets each. Elinor says she has three pets. Tymar says she has fewer pets than anyone else. Eve says she has three pets. Ben says he has more pets than anyone else. How many pets can Tymar and Ben have each?

   .... 2 marks

Answers

MEASURES

1 Length
1. b) David, by 30 cm
2. Mozart (96 mm), Brahms (145 mm), Beethoven (550 mm)
3. a) post box
   b) dentist
   c) newsagent

2 Weight
1. b) 2.5 kg   c) £2
2. long grain (2,000 g), basmati (1,750 g), jasmine (1,500 g), brown (650 g)
3. a) Standard van by 100 kg
   b) Less than the four-wheel drive by 200 kg and less than the standard by 300 kg

3 Volume and capacity
1. b) 12.5 litres
2. 50 days
3. a) No, 750 ml is less than 1 litre as 1 litre is 1000 ml
   b) 150 ml

4 Reading scales
1. b) 240 g   c) 460 g   d) 68 °F
2. Jug A contains 300 ml and jug B contains 260 ml so jug A contains more liquid.

5 Converting units
1. b) 1,320 mm   c) 36.84 m   d) 85.72 m
   e) 6.734 litres   f) 8.243 litres
2. 6,250 g
3. 4,445 ml or 4.445 litres
4. a) 1,400 g   b) 170 ml

6 Ordering measures
1. 5 cm, 168 mm, 56 cm, 2.5 m, 18 m, 11 km
2. 482 ml, 672 ml, $\frac{3}{4}$ litres, $\frac{4}{5}$ litres, 930 ml, 13 litres
3. 300 g, 2,500 g, 3 kg, 4 kg, 16 kg, 44 kg
4. a) true   b) false   c) false
5. b) <   c) >

7 Calculating with measures
1. b) 1,080 g   c) 1.08 kg
2. 3.571 litres
3. 10.4 m
4. 50.3 km
5. 1,400 g

8 Imperial units
1. b) 64
2. a) 13,500   b) 20
3. 2,250 ml
4. a) 56 km   b) 624 km

9 Time
1. b) five minutes past one in the afternoon
2. a) half past ten in the evening
   b) five minutes to two in the morning
3. a) 1 hour and 5 minutes
   b) 26 mins
   c) 9 mins

10 Money
1. b) £9   c) £4.80
2. a) £1.35   b) £0.75   c) £1.40   d) 20

11 Perimeter and area
1. b) perimeter = 14 cm, area = 12 cm²
2. 14 cm
3. 2 cm × 3 cm
4. The diagonal lines are longer than 1 cm (or any acceptable explanation)

12 Compound shapes
1. b) perimeter = 30 cm, area = 26 cm²
   c) perimeter = 32 cm, area = 23 cm²
   d) perimeter = 22 cm, area = 17 cm²

13 Areas of triangles
1. b) 6 cm²
2. a) Sophia is correct. The area of each triangle is $\frac{1}{2}$ × base length × perpendicular height, which is 3 units × 4 units = 6 units² for all three triangles.
   b) There are lots of correct answers. Your triangle should have a base length of 3 units and a height of 4 units or a base length of 4 units and a height of 3 units.

14 Areas of parallelograms
1. b) 56 cm²
2. shape A and shape D
3. No, Lydia is incorrect. For example, a parallelogram with base length 4 cm and perpendicular height 2 cm has area 8 cm² but the lengths of the two straight sides add up to 8 cm so the perimeter must be greater than 8 cm.

15 Volumes of cuboids
1. b) 144 cm³   c) 336 cm³
2. 180 m³
3. 3 cm
4. Statement B is true. The cuboid could be a cube with dimensions 3 × 3 × 3 but it could also be a cuboid with dimensions 9 × 3 × 1

GEOMETRY

16 Triangles and quadrilaterals
1. B and D
2. rhombus
3. 56 cm

Answers

17 Circles
1. 30 cm²
2. 4.5 cm
3. 12 cm

18 Other 2D shapes
1. b) F   c) E   d) B
2. a) C   b) A   c) E

19 Properties of 2D shapes
1. a) The perimeters of the shapes are the same.
   b) The areas of the shapes are the same.
2. 20 cm
3. a) For example:

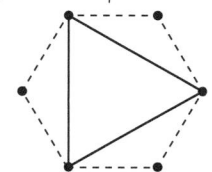

   b) For example:

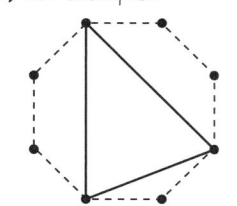

4. E

20 Drawing 2D shapes
1. 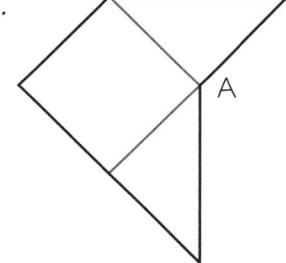
2. For example: 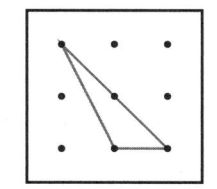
3. 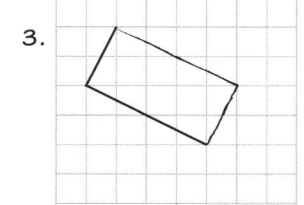
4.

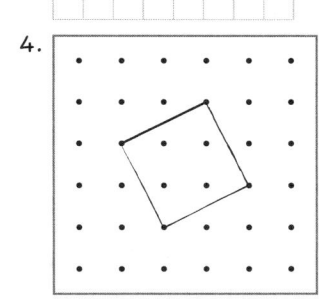

21 Naming 3D shapes
1. first shape: cube
   second shape: square-based pyramid
   third shape: cuboid
   fourth shape: hexagonal prism
2. a) sphere   b) cylinder   c) tetrahedron
3. triangular prism

22 Nets
1. ticks for the first and third nets
2. 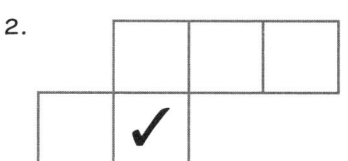
3. 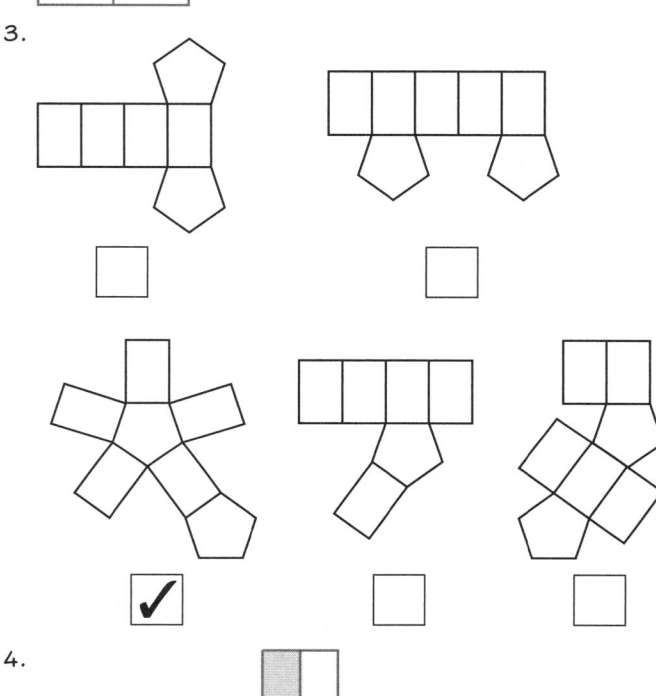
4.

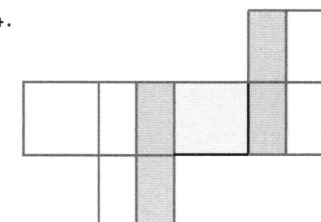

23 Angles
1. C, A, B, D
2. a and d
3. C and D
4.
5. The angles in a triangle always add up to 180°. Obtuse angles are greater than 90° and 90 + 90 = 180 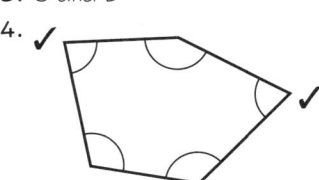
   This means Boyd can't be correct because two obtuse angles add up to more than 180°.

24 Measuring angles
1. b) 32°, acute   c) 99°, obtuse   d) 341°, reflex
2. lions 118°, tigers 100°, bears 92°, monkeys 50°

40

Answers

25 Finding unknown angles
1. 270°
2. 35°
3. 25°
4. a = 55°, b = 145°

26 Coordinates
1. (4, 3)
2. [graph showing a tilted square with vertices at approximately (3,2), (4,5), (7,4), (6,1)]
3. (5, 4)

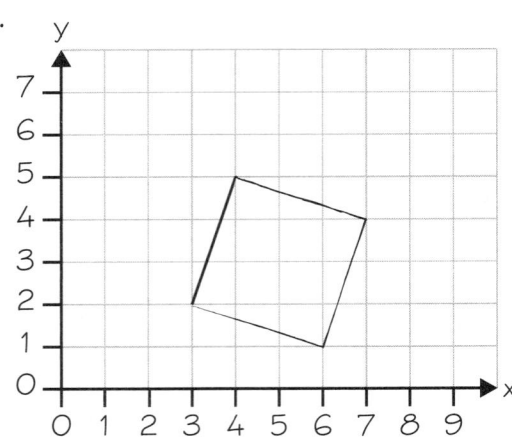

27 Translation
1. a) [graph showing shaded square in upper left quadrant and square in lower right quadrant]
   b) [graph showing square in lower left quadrant and shaded rectangle in upper right quadrant]
3. b) 3 squares right and 6 squares down

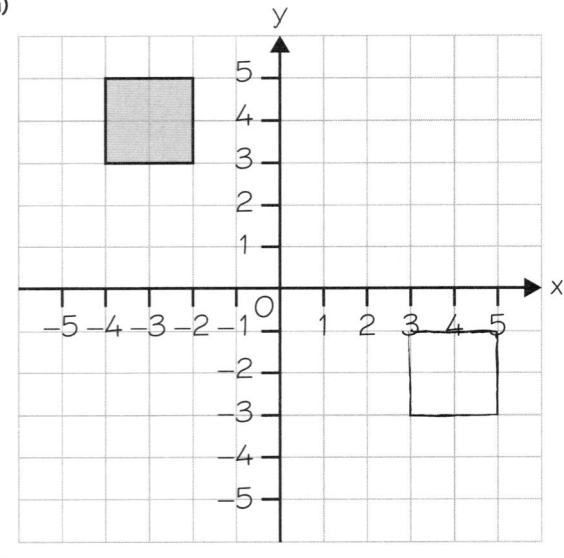

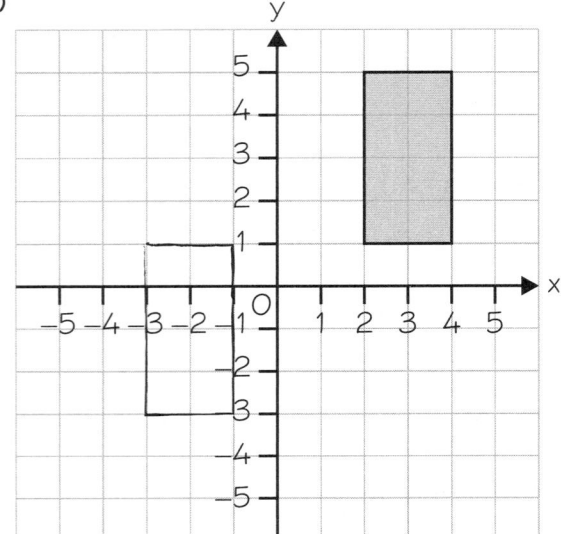

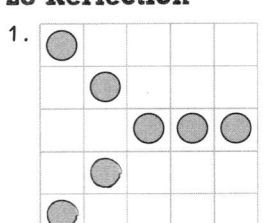

28 Reflection
1. [grid showing reflected pattern of circles]
2. Shapes 1, 3 and 4 are ticked.
3. a) [reflected arrow/chevron shapes across vertical dashed line]
   b) [shapes reflected across diagonal dashed line]
4. [graph showing L-shapes reflected across the y-axis]

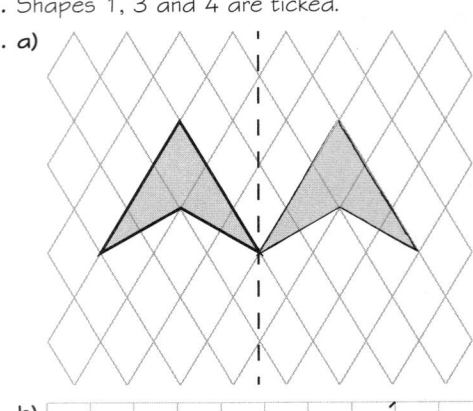

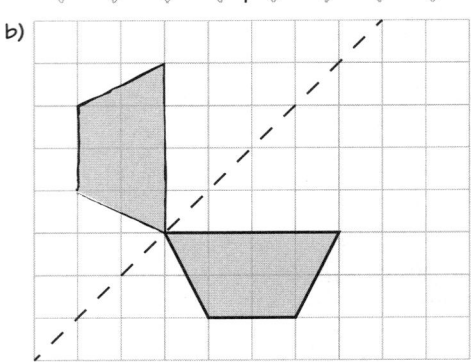

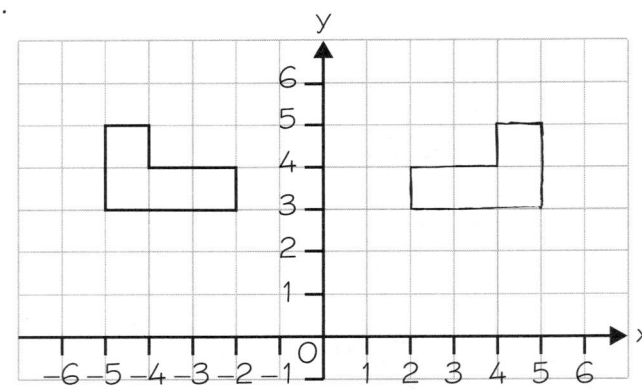

STATISTICS

29 Tables
1. b) Theo   c) 8 cm
2. a) Chris and Ophelia   b) Ophelia   c) Usy
3. a) Henry   b) Fiona and Susha

30 Timetables
1. b) 50 minutes   c) 13:15
2. a) 36 minutes   b) 14:04   c) 14:55

31 Bar charts
1. b) 6   c) 2   d) 24
2. a) 14   b) 26   c) 48

41

Answers

32 Drawing bar charts

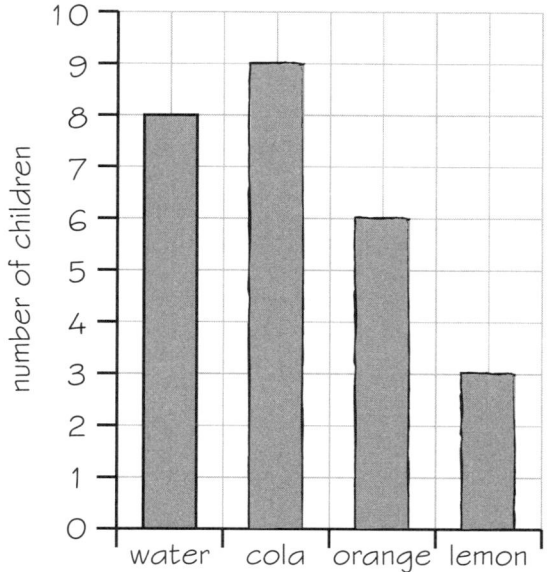

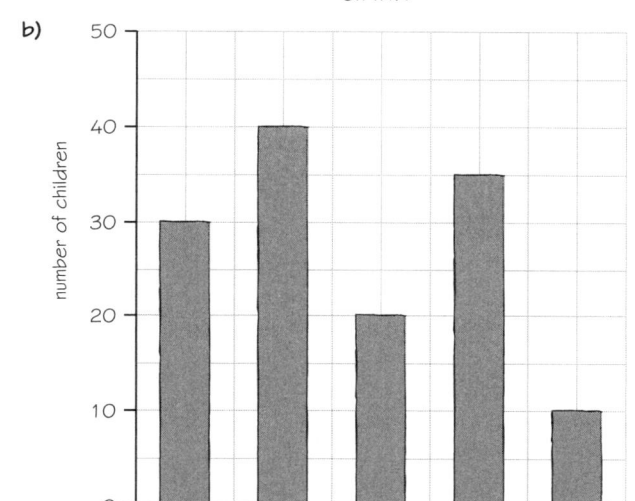

1. a) [Bar chart: water 8, cola 9, orange 6, lemon 3; y-axis: number of children, x-axis: drink]

   b) [Bar chart: apples 30, bananas 40, grapes 20, oranges 35, pears 10; y-axis: number of children, x-axis: favourite fruit]

33 Pie charts

1. b) Thursday   c) Wednesday
2. a) 120   b) one quarter
   c) No – the fractions for these are the same, so the same number travelled by bike as by car.

34 Drawing pie charts

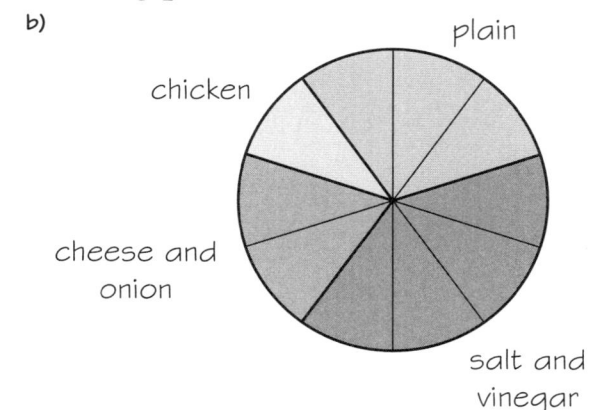

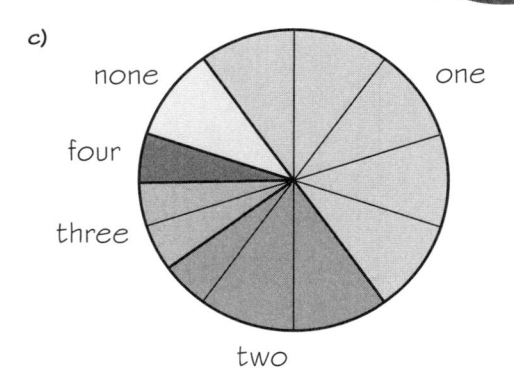

b) [Pie chart with sections labelled: plain, chicken, cheese and onion, salt and vinegar]

c) [Pie chart with sections labelled: none, one, two, three, four]

35 Line graphs

a) Ghalib 8 a.m., Sam 9 a.m.
b) 10 a.m.
c) i) 1 hour   ii) 25 km   iii) 11.30 a.m.
d) The last stage, between 1.30 and 2 p.m.
e) No, they both finished at the same time.

36 Drawing line graphs

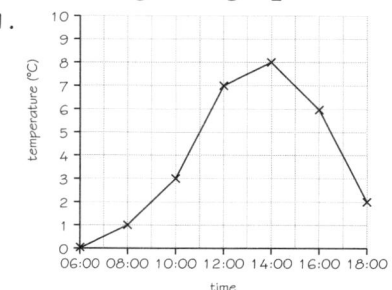

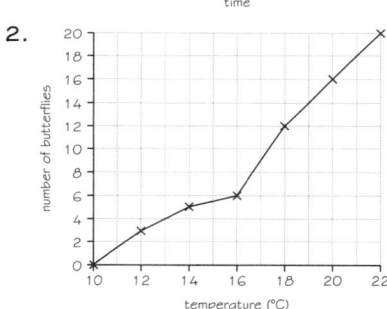

1. [Line graph: temperature (°C) vs time from 06:00 to 18:00]

2. [Line graph: number of butterflies vs temperature (°C) from 10 to 22]

37 Calculating the mean

1. b) 6 kg   c) 43p
2. a) 1 point
   b) No, he lost ten points which could have been 2 games lost with 2 games drawn.

38 Using the mean

1. 81
2. 7
3. 112 cm
4. Tymar has no pets and Ben has 6 pets **or**
   Tymar has 1 pet and Ben has 5 pets **or**
   Tymar has 2 pets and Ben has 4 pets.

Published by Pearson Education Limited, 80 Strand, London, WC2R 0RL.

www.pearsonschools.co.uk

Text © Pearson Education Limited 2016
Edited by Christine Vaughan
Typeset by Jouve India Private Limited
Produced by Elektra Media
Original illustrations © Pearson Education Limited 2016
Illustrated by Elektra Media
Cover illustration by Ana Albero

The rights of Christopher Bishop and Brian Speed to be identified as authors of this work have been asserted by them in accordance with the Copyright, Designs and Patents Act 1988.

First published 2016

19 18 17 16
10 9 8 7 6 5 4 3 2 1

British Library Cataloguing in Publication Data
A catalogue record for this book is available from the British Library.

ISBN 978 1 292 14622 5

Copyright notice
All rights reserved. No part of this publication may be reproduced in any form or by any means (including photocopying or storing it in any medium by electronic means and whether or not transiently or incidentally to some other use of this publication) without the written permission of the copyright owner, except in accordance with the provisions of the Copyright, Designs and Patents Act 1988 or under the terms of a licence issued by the Copyright Licensing Agency, Barnard's Inn, 86 Fetter Lane, London EC4A 1EN (www.cla.co.uk). Applications for the copyright owner's written permission should be addressed to the publisher.

Printed in Italy by L.E.G.O. S.p.A.